P9-ELT-714

New Comic Limericks

New Comic Limericks

Laughable Poems by Ogden Nash, Edward Lear,
Charles Barsotti, Dean Walley, and Others

Edited by Ivanette Dennis

Illustrated by Louis Marak

HALLMARK EDITIONS

New Comic Limericks

A cute secretary, none cuter,
Was replaced by a clicking computer.
    T'was the wife of her boss
    Who put this deal across;
You see, the computer was neuter.

Ogden Nash

A magician of Kalamazoo
Said, "There's nothing that I cannot do.
   It's the Fourth of July,
   But why should we fry?
Let it snow! Let it snow!"—And it snew.

Ogden Nash

Returned from their first trip to Mars,
The explorers all headed for bars—
   "The 'canals' that we dared
   Left us terribly scared—
Those aren't people up there, they're cars!"

Richard Rhodes

There was a young lady of Florence,
Who for kissing professed great abhorrence;
    But when she'd been kissed
    And found what she'd missed,
She cried till the tears came in torrents.

Anonymous

Count Dracula said to his pal:
"Say, Frank, what you need is a gal,
    And I know a young dear
    Who's been dead for a year
So she'll surely improve your morale."

Ed Cunningham

A rare old bird is the pelican,
His beak holds more than his belican.
    He can take in his beak
    Enough food for a week.
I'm darned if I know how the helican!

Dixon Merritt

As the natives got ready to serve
A midget explorer named Merve,
   "This meal will be brief,"
   Said the cannibal chief,
"For the chap is at most an hors d'oeuvre!"

Ed Cunningham

A jolly young fellow from Yuma
Told an elephant joke to a puma.
   Now his skeleton lies
   Under hot western skies.
The puma had no sense of huma.

Ogden Nash

There once was a boy in Quebec,
Who was buried in snow to his neck.
   When asked, "Are you friz?"
   He replied, "Yes, I is,
But we don't call this cold in Quebec."

Rudyard Kipling

Adam was surprisingly glib
When he discovered he'd lost a rib:
    "I can't conceive
    How to use Eve
But I sure like the cut of her jib!"

                    Charles Barsotti

A certain young chap named Bill Beebee
Was in love with a lady named Phoebe.
    "But," said he, "I must see
    What the clerical fee
Be before Phoebe be Phoebe B. Beebee."

                    Author Unknown

There once was a cutie named Sunny
Whose ears were so long it was funny.
    But don't moan her fate
    For the gal's doing great—
She's a key club's most popular bunny!

Mary Rita Hurley

God's plan made a hopeful beginning
But man spoiled his chances by sinning.
    We trust that the story
    Will end in God's glory;
But, at present, the other side's winning.

Oliver Wendell Holmes

I once thought a lot of a friend
Who turned out to be in the end
    (As I'd feared at the start)
    The southernmost part
Of a horse with a northerly trend.

Anonymous

A stubborn young bachelor named Boze
Took an oath that he'd never propose.
    He spent his sad life
    Without taking a wife,
Till in bed one cold winter, Boze froze!

Barbara Burrow

There was an old man of Thermopylae,
Who never did anything properly;
    But they said: "If you choose
    To boil eggs in your shoes,
You cannot remain in Thermopylae."

Edward Lear

An old Indian named Running B'ar
At making it rain was a star.
    Asked, "How do you do it?"
    He said, "Nothing to it—
To get rain, me just wash-um car!"

Mary Rita Hurley

A cat in despondency sighed,
And resolved to commit suicide;
    She passed under the wheels
    Of eight automobiles,
And after the ninth one she died.

Anonymous

There once was a maid with such graces,
That her curves cried aloud for embraces.
    "You look," cried each he,
    "Like a million to me—
Invested in all the right places!"

Author Unknown

There was a hillbilly named Shaw
Who envied his maw and his paw.
    To share in their life
    He adopted his wife
And became his own father-in-law.

Ogden Nash

There were three little birds in a wood,
Who always sang hymns when they could;
    What the words were about
    They could never make out,
But they felt it was doing them good.

Author Unknown

An old millionaire of Fort Worth
When asked for the cause of his mirth
    Replied, "Houston and Dallas
    Will shore bust a gallus
When they hear I've just purchased the earth."

Ogden Nash

There once was a gal from Calais
Who wandered a little astray,
    Not by smoking or drinking
    And not what you're thinking—
She got lost on the Rue de la Paix.

Mary Rita Hurley

Van Allen's Belt, at first glance
Seems to cover a mighty expanse—
    But a belt in the sky
    Leaves me wondering why
No mention is made of the pants!

Charles Barsotti

An old Danish jester named Yorick
Drank a gallon of pure paregoric.
    "My jokes have been dull,"
    Said he, "but my skull
Will one of these days be historic."

Ogden Nash

That inept young lass, Miss Muffet
Had further bad luck with her tuffet:
    Some used-tuffet dealers
    Decided to steal hers,
And now she must rent one or rough it!

Dean Walley

There was a young lady named Bianca
Who slept while her ship lay at anchor.
    She awoke in dismay
    When she heard the mate say:
"Hi! Hoist up the top-sheet and spanker!"

Author Unknown

A newspaper reader quite sage
Would go into a terrible rage
    When he would choose
    To read some big news
And find it (continued)

19

next page!

Charles Barsotti

A student who lived in Montmartre
Had studied more Descartes than Sartre.
  He said, "What's essential
  Is not Existential,
But 'We think, and therefore we artre'."

William Peterson

There was a young fellow named Sydney,
Who drank till he ruined his kidney.
  It shriveled and shrank,
  As he sat there and drank,
But he had lots of fun doin' it, didney?

Don Marquis

There was an old fellow named Green,
Who grew so abnormally lean,
    And flat, and compressed,
    That his back squeezed his chest,
And sideways he couldn't be seen.

Anonymous

While sailing his ark, Captain Noah
Had an angry exchange with a boa.
    For excessive constricting
    Noah threatened evicting,
But the boa pledged Noah "no mo'a!"

Dean Walley

There was a young lady in white
Who looked out at the depths of the night;
    But the birds of the air
     Filled her heart with despair,
And oppressed that young lady in white.

Edward Lear

A famous bullfighter named Zeke
Pleased the crowds with his casual technique.
    Each time he was gored
    He just acted bored,
Pausing only to plug up the leak.

Dean Walley

There once was a spaceman named Wright,
Whose speed was much faster than light.
    He set out one day,
    In a relative way,
And returned on the previous night.

Author Unknown

24

A fly and a flea in a flue
Were imprisoned, so what could they do?
    Said the fly, "Let us flee!"
    "Let us fly!" said the flea.
So they flew through a flaw in the flue.

Author Unknown

There was a young fellow named Weir,
Who hadn't an atom of fear;
    He indulged a desire
    To touch a live wire;
—Now any last line will do here.

Anonymous

There was a young lady from Cork
Who tackled her soup with a fork.
    When her parents looked pained,
    She proudly explained,
"That's the way they eat soup in New York."

Ogden Nash

There was a young fellow named Fisher,
Who was fishing for fish in a fissure,
    When a cod with a grin
    Pulled the fisherman in...
Now they're fishing the fissure for Fisher.

Author Unknown

There was a young lady named Munn
Who clobbered her boy friend in fun,
    Saying, "Don't worry, kid,
    That's for nothing you did,
Just for something I dreamt that you done."

Ogden Nash

There once was a pious young priest,
Who lived almost wholly on yeast;
    "For," he said, "it is plain
    We must all rise again,
And I want to get started at least."

Anonymous

There once was a fellow named Brian
Who was bitten one day by a lion.
    He went on the prowl
    And he started to growl,
But other than that he's just fion.

        Mary Volk

There was a young belle of old Natchez
Whose garments were always in patchez.
    When comment arose
    On the state of her clothes,
She drawled, "When Ah itchez, Ah scratchez!"

        Ogden Nash

The Reverend Henry Ward Beecher
Called a hen a most elegant creature.
    The hen, pleased with that,
    Laid an egg in his hat—
And thus did the hen reward Beecher.

Oliver Wendell Holmes

An old maid, a luckless romantic,
Said, as she crossed the Atlantic:
    "Now is my chance
    To find true romance
On this beautiful ship, the Titanic!"

William Peterson

A bugler named Dougal MacDougal
Found ingenious ways to be frugal.
    He learned how to sneeze
    In appropriate keys
Thus saving the price of a bugle.

Ogden Nash

An insurance salesman named Flint
Said with a satisfied squint,
    "Don't try to collect—
    You ought to have checked—
I excluded that clause in small print."

Charles Barsotti

The story is sadly repeated,
That Sid thought he was painfully treated,
    But you must agree that
    When on cactus Sid sat,
His cause of complaint was deep-seated.

Mary Rita Hurley

There once was a silly young maid
Who only ate grape marmalade.
    At one hundred and ten
    She said with a grin,
"How nicely preserved I have stayed!"

Author Unknown

A young rock-and-roller named Clyde
Always kept his guitar by his side;
    All night he kept strumming
    And never stopped humming,
'Til he ran out of rhythm and died.

Dean Walley

An elderly bridegroom named Purvis
Grew quite justifiably nurvis
    When he caught his young wife
    Insuring his life
Immediately after the survis.

Ogden Nash

There once was a werewolf in Rome
Who lived in an old catacomb.
    No gastronomical purist,
    He gobbled up tourists,
Small cars, shoes, and old Kodachrome!

Charles Barsotti

I'd rather have fingers than toes;
I'd rather have ears than a nose;
    And as for my hair,
    I'm glad it's all there,
And I will be sad when it goes.

Gelett Burgess

Asked a patient who faced appendectomy,
"What kind of a fee d'you expectomy?"
    Said the doc, "Since your pulse
    Indicates the results,
Any kind but a post-dated checktomy."

Ogden Nash

33

There was an old miner named Crane
Who used dynamite sticks for a cane.
    They found his hat
    On Mount Arrat
And part of his bridgework in Spain.

Richard Rhodes

There was a young lady named Jeanie
Who wore an outrageous bikini,
    Two wisps light as air,
    One here and one there,
With nothing but Jeanie betweenie.

Ogden Nash

Consider the plight of poor Jim,
Who, when asked what girl was for him,
    Said, "A tramp or a lady
    Twixt thirteen and eighty,
Dumb, smart, short, tall, fat or slim!"

Ed Cunningham

A limerick writer from Liddle
Would ponder and puzzle and fiddle—
    Da dum da da dum
    Da dum da da dum—
He could end and begin, but not middle!

Charles Barsotti

A confident sailor named Harris
Was navigator aboard a Polaris,
    But his aim was bizarre
    And his sub sailed so far
It came up in the Seine north of Paris!

Karen Becraft

There was a young girl of Milwaukee
Whose voice was so squeaky and squawky
    That her friends were emphatic
    It sounded like static,
And called her their Milwaukee-talkie.

Ogden Nash

There was a young fellow named Fonda
Who was squeezed by a large anaconda.
    Now he's only a smear
    With part of him here
And the rest of him somewhere out yonda.

Ogden Nash

There was a young person from Perth
Who was born on the day of his birth.
    He was married, they say,
    On his wife's wedding day,
And died when he quitted this earth.

Author Unknown

As an acrobat Clyde was no whiz,
But undying fame is now his;
    When his trapeze broke down
    He won great renown:
He screamed as he fell, "That's show biz!"

Ed Cunningham

A certain old maid of Cohoes,
In despair, taught her bird to propose;
    But the parrot, dejected
    At being accepted,
Spoke some words too profane to disclose.

Author Unknown

There was a young maid of Ostend,
Who swore she'd hold out to the end;
    But alas! half-way over,
    'Twixt Calais and Dover,
She'd done what she didn't intend.

Author Unknown

A caveman named Agar Ageel
Cried out with historical zeal:
    "I'm the first man alive
    Who can go for a drive

Charles Barsotti

A poet who belonged in a cage

Thought limericks to be all the rage,

But part of his charm Was to forget about form,

And run 'round the edge of the page!

Charles Barsotti

There once was a lady named Erskine
Who had a remarkable fair skin.
 When I said to her, "Mabel,
 You'd look well in sable."
She answered, "I'm best in my bearskin."

Author Unknown

There once was a postman named Hale
Who swam into the mouth of a whale.
 He looked all about
 Crying, "Jonah, come out,
There's one cent postage due on your mail!"

Ogden Nash

Said an astronaut stuck in his Gemini,
"I'm afraid, as things stand presently,
 The latch on the hatch
 Has a catch that won't catch—
And the view may be getting more heavenly."

Richard Rhodes

"My job's an imbecility
With this verbal disability:
    I doubt if I ever can
    Be a good weatherman
Stammering pre-pre-precipitation
    pro-pro-probability."

Richard Rhodes

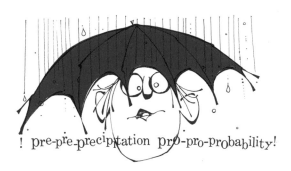

! pre-pre-precipitation pro-pro-probability!

A botany major named Grant
Chanced to swallow a man-eating plant.
    Now he says his interior
    Feels rather inferior,
And his chance for survival is scant.

Dean Walley

A girl who weighed many an oz.
Used language I dare not pronoz.
    For a fellow unkind
    Pulled her chair out behind
Just to see (so he said) if she'd boz.

P. L. Mannock

There was an old man of the Cape
Who made himself garments of crepe.
    When asked, "Do they tear?"
    He replied, "Here and there;
But they're perfectly splendid for shape."

Robert Louis Stevenson

There was an odd fellow of Tyre,
Who constantly sat on the fire.
    When asked, "Are you hot?"
    He said, "Certainly not.
I'm James Winterbotham, Esquire."

Anonymous

43

I wish that my room had a floor;
I don't care very much for a door,
    But this walking around
    Without touching the ground
Is getting to be such a bore.

Gelett Burgess

A buxom young lady of France
Wore the tightest of form-fitting pants.
    When she stooped in the bank
    To pick up a franc
The form-fitting pants were ex-panse.

Ogden Nash

Turning over a new leaf would pose
No problem for most, except those
    Who like the first Adam
    And his ambitious madam
Use only new leaves for their clothes.

Patricia White

A skillful shoplifter named Herring
Plied his art with admirable daring:
    He stole ermine and pearls,
    Thirteen salesgirls,
And the clothes the floorwalker was wearing.

Dean Walley

An amoeba named Sam, and his brother,
Were having a drink with each other;
    In the midst of their quaffing
    They split their sides laughing
And each of them now is a mother.

Author Unknown

A maiden arrested in Deeming
For attire that was most unbeseeming
    The queen of the ball—
    Just a crown and that's all—
Said, "Good Heavens,
I thought I was dreaming!"

Anonymous

There once was a gnu in the zoo
Who tired of the same daily view.
    To seek a new sight
    He stole out one night—
But where he went gnobody gnu!

Patricia White

A lawyer you won't want to meet
Believed no question was moot.
    When the judge charged, "The Savior
    Disbarred your behavior,"
He said smugly, "*My* eye has no mote."

George Nolan

There was a young lady, Miss White
Who in drinking took excess delight.
    When they told her she shouldn't
    She said, "Stop! Oh, I couldn't—
I only feel right when I'm tight!"

Anonymous

No lady goes out without gloves
Nor whispers bad things of her loves,
    And if she is aging
    Her form's more engaging
Held in firmly below and aboves.

Arthur Stanley

An espionage agent named Strode
Had quite an unusual code:
    Each message he sent
    Was twisted and bent,
Then tattooed on the tongue of a toad.

Dean Walley

There was a young lady from Lynn
Who was sunk in original sin.
    When they said, "Do be good,"
    She replied, "If I could...
But I'd do wrong right over again."

Anonymous

A lovely young maiden named Carol
At Niagara donned swimming apparel.
    We heard from the shore,
    "Oh, swimming's a bore!"
So she went down the falls in a barrel!

Charles Barsotti

There was a young lady from Rye
With a shape like a capital I.
    When they said, "It's too bad,"
    She learned how to pad,
Which shows you that figures can lie.

Author Unknown

In Japan a fat tourist from Surrey
Ate his curry in too great a hurry.
    He stuffed like a goat
    Till it stuck in his throat.
The coroner said, "Hurri-kurri."

Ogden Nash

There once was a gay caballero
Who was losing his loot playing faro
    Then he vowed he would eat
    His hat, were he beat—
Have you ever tried french-fried sombrero?

Dean Walley

A scholar who feared to misquote
Carefully clarified all that he wrote.
    His works were well padded
    With each reference added*

There was a young man of Japan,
Who wrote verses that never would scan,
    When they said, "But the thing
    Doesn't go with a swing,"
He said, "Yes, but I always like to get
    as many words into the last line
    as I possibly can."

Anonymous

*In the form of a learned footnote.

Charles Barsotti

There was a young athlete named Tribbling
Whose hobby was basketball dribbling,
But he dribbled one day
On a busy freeway —
Now his sister is missing a sibling!

Dean Walley

There was an old man of Dumbree,
Who taught little owls to drink tea;
For he said, "To eat mice,
Is not proper or nice,"
That amiable man of Dumbree.

Edward Lear

There was a faith-healer of Deal,
Who said, "Although pain isn't real,
    If I sit on a pin
    And it punctures my skin,
I dislike what I fancy I feel."

Author Unknown

A careless explorer named Blake
Fell into a tropical lake.
 Said a fat alligator
 A few minutes later,
"Very nice, but I still prefer steak."

Ogden Nash

A diner while dining at Crew
Found a rather large mouse in his stew.
 Said the waiter, "Don't shout
 And wave it about,
Or the rest will be wanting one, too."

Anonymous

A bottle of perfume that Willie sent
Was highly displeasing to Millicent.
    Her thanks were so cold
    That they quarreled, I'm told,
Of that silly scent Willie sent Millicent.

Anonymous

A scientist from dark Transylvania
Said, "I certainly hate to detain ya,
    But my son Frankenstein
    Needs an ear and a spine,
And I don't think
    their loss would much pain ya!"

Charles Barsotti

The sermon our Pastor Rt. Rev.
Began, may have had a rt. clev.,
    But his talk, though consistent,
    Kept the end so far distant
That we left, since we felt he mt. nev.

Author Unknown

There was an old person of Bromley,
Whose ways were not cheerful nor comely;
    He sat in the dust,
    Eating spiders and crust,
That unpleasing old person of Bromley.

Edward Lear

In Egypt resides the old Sphinx
Who sits in the sun and just thinks —
    Of dark Ptolemy,
    Of Rameses III,
And of Kool-Aid and other cold drinks.

William Peterson

There was a young lady named Flo
Who was padded from top-knot to toe.
    She was hit by a truck,
    Which was very poor luck—
She's still bouncing as far as we know.

Anonymous

A cigarette fiend from Bryn Mawr
Declined an expensive cigar.
    "Tobacco," said she,
    "Means nothing to me,
I smoke cigarettes for the tar."

Ogden Nash

A poet named Phineas McBurch
Carved a verse on the pew of a church.
    In his wrath, the Rector
    Invoked the Protector,
And McBurch left the church in a lurch.

Arthur Stanley

There once was a barber named Ware
Who was sadly allergic to hair.
   When customers called,
   Unless they were bald,
He would sneeze them right out of the chair.

Ogden Nash

"Please excuse my bad dancing," said he,
"I'm stiff from bowling, you see."
   Said the girl, "As to where
   You are from, I don't care—
Just please stop stepping on me!"

Patricia White

Of neighbors, the less heard the better,
And stave off your in-laws by letter,
    But when grandchildren visit,
    Their constant "What is it?"
Is answered much better by fetter.

Arthur Stanley

An ancient eccentric of Broome
Kept an ugly baboon in his room.
    "It reminds me," he said,
    Of a friend who is dead."
But he refused to tell us of whom.

Anonymous

A tone-deaf old person from Tring
When somebody asked him to sing,
    Replied "It is odd
    But I cannot tell *God*
Save the Weasel from *Pop Goes the King.*"

Author Unknown

A fellow named William John Lew
Got more hairy each year as he grew.
    Unable one day
    To shave it away
He screamed, "Call me Winnie-the-Pooh!"

Anonymous

An accented youth of Cologne
With a pain in his stomach did mogne.
    He heaved a great sigh
    And said, "I would digh,
But the loss would be only my ogne."

Author Unknown

A brave but quite odd gladiator
Fell in love with a young alligator.
    His friends said, "You fool,
    Get out of that pool,
You're expected to fight her, not date her!"

Dean Walley

There was a young girl of Tacoma
Who rejected her sheepskin diploma.
   She knew it was made with
   A lamb she had played with
And recognized by the aroma.

Ogden Nash

A certain young man from East Gluver
Was a most ardent limerick lover.
   When he came to this part
   He read back to the start
From cover to cover to cover.

Dean Walley

Designed by Carole Muller.

Set in photocomposed Caledonia,
a 20th century roman typeface
with Scottish modifications.
Printed on Hallmark Eggshell Book paper.